Letter Challenge

arn to Form Letters and Symbols Correctly with Art and Puzzle Games

30 GAMES

A Unique Way to Teach Writing to Active and Creative Kids.

The Thinking Tree

The Thinking TREE

www.DyslexiaGames.com

Dyslexia Games Series A - Book 3
Friendly Copyright Notice:

The Thinking Tree LLC   ●   617 N Swope St.   ●   Greenfield, IN 46140   ●   info@dyslexiagames.com   ●   (317) 622-885

Letter Challenge

Learn to form letters and symbols correctly with Art and Puzzle Games

By Sarah J. Brown

Parent Teacher Instructions:

Provide the student with a set of sharp colored pencils or colorful markers, and a fine point black pen.

These lessons tap into your child's natural problem solving skills, so he may not need much assistance. You may want to work with your child on pages 25 –29. These pages cover letter formation based on the Distar Reading Program, and the book "Teach Your Child to Read in 100 Easy Lessons".

These exercises develop handwriting skills, precision, proper letter formation, tracking skills, thinking skills, and reading skills.

Children learn to write letters, words and numbers while tapping into the creative area of their minds.

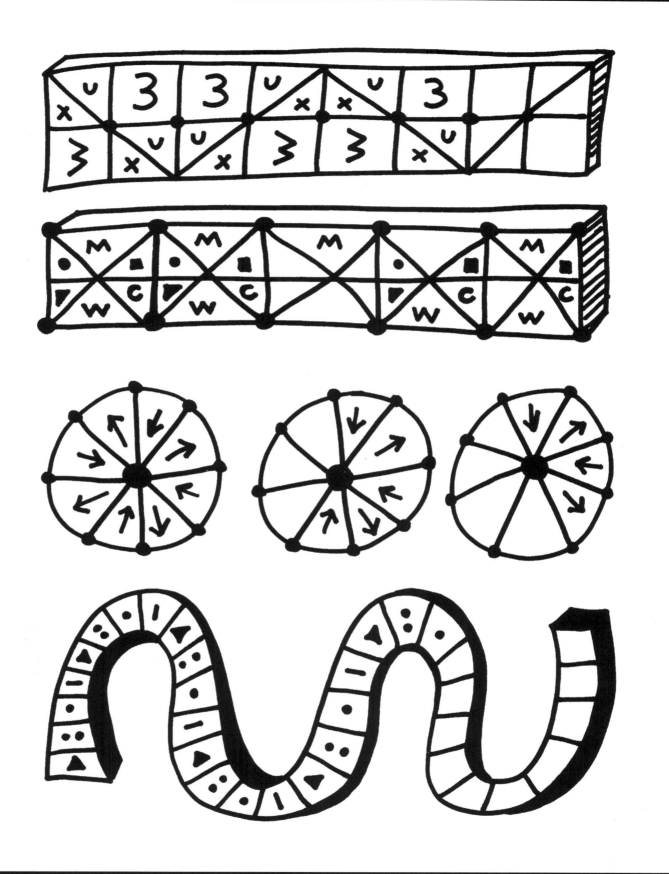

Name:_____   Date:_____

Name:_____ **Date:**_____

Name:_____   **Date:**_____

Name:_____   **Date:**_____

Name:_____   **Date:**_____

Name:_____   Date:_____

flower pot

Name:_____ Date:_____

Name:_____ **Date:**_____

Name:_____ **Date:**_____

Name:_____   **Date:**_____

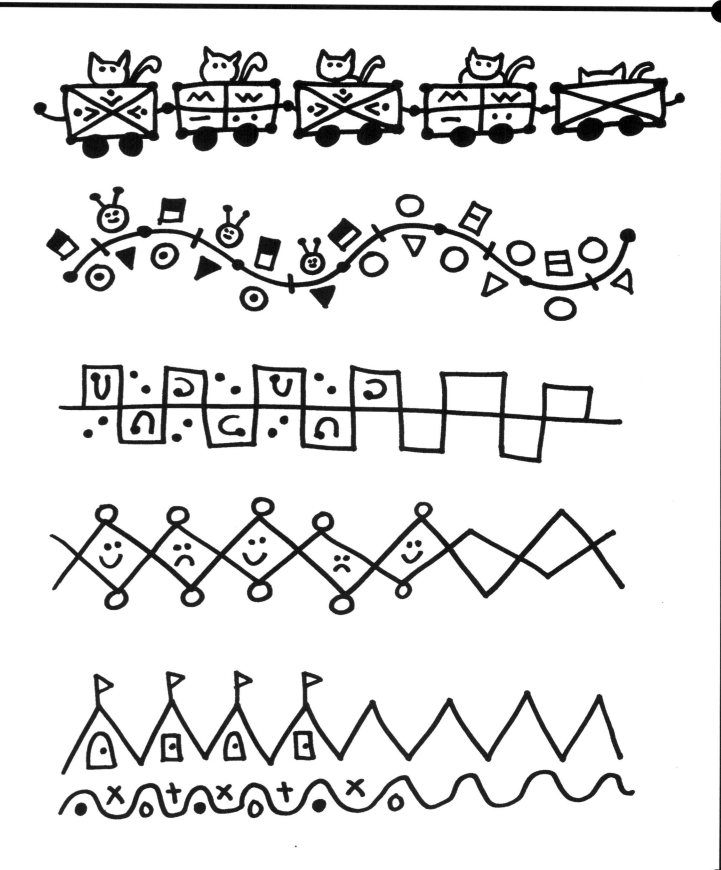

Name:_____ **Date:**_____

Name:_____   Date:_____

Name:_____ **Date:**_____

Name:_____   **Date:**_____

Name:_____ **Date:**_____

Name:_____   Date:_____

Name:_____ **Date:**_____

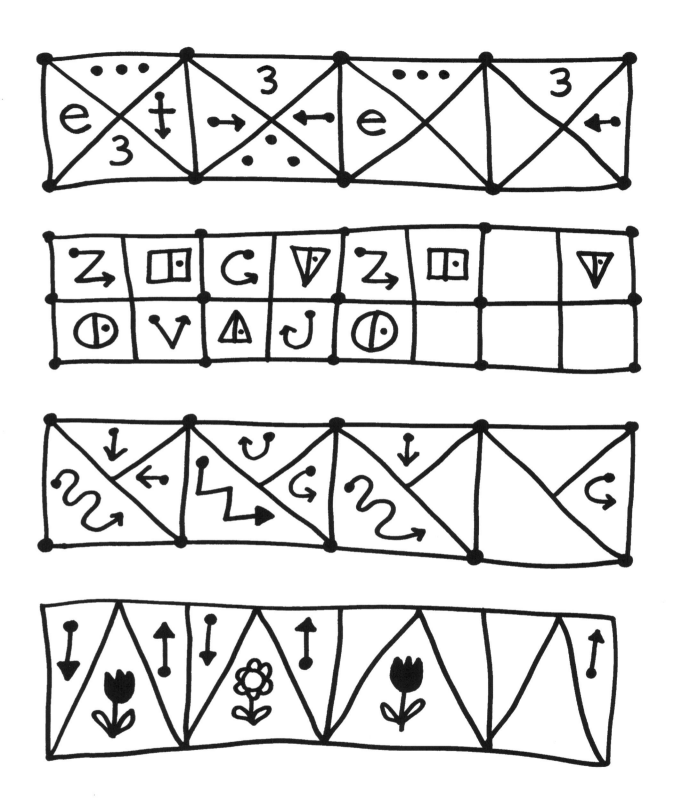

Name:_____   Date:_____

Name:_____ **Date:**_____

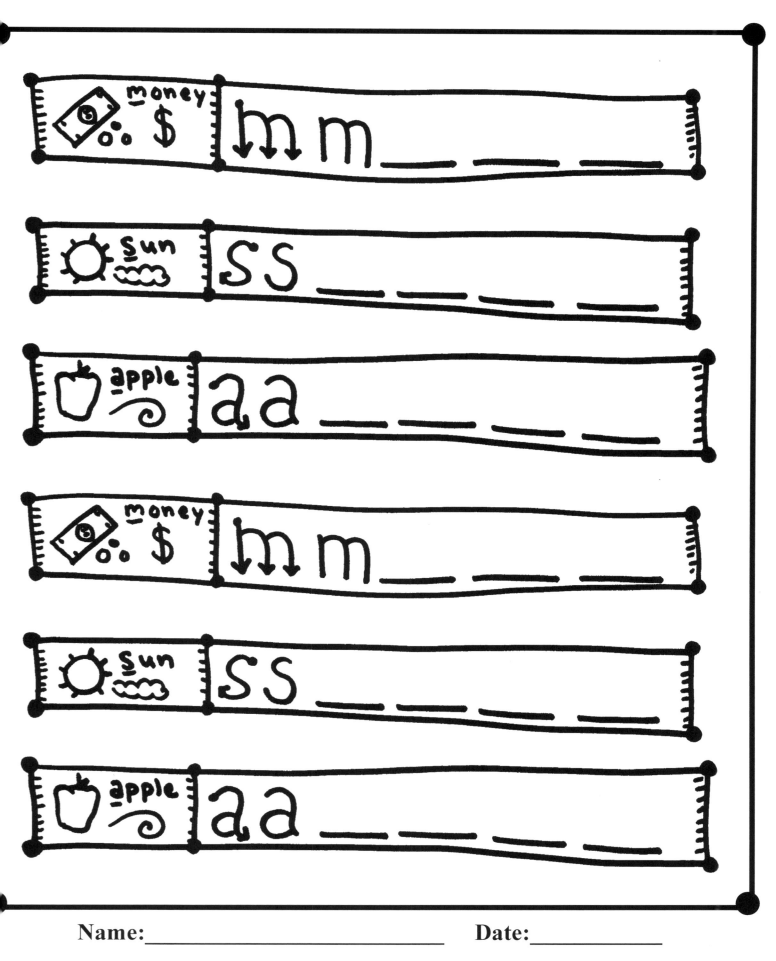

Name:_____ **Date:**_____

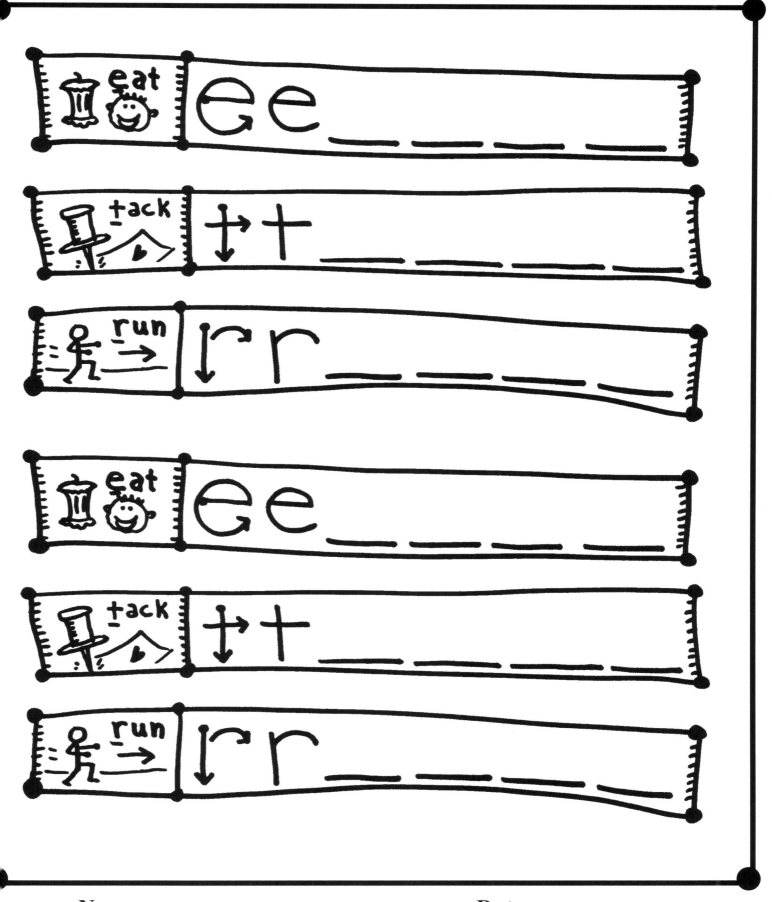

Name:_____   **Date:**_____

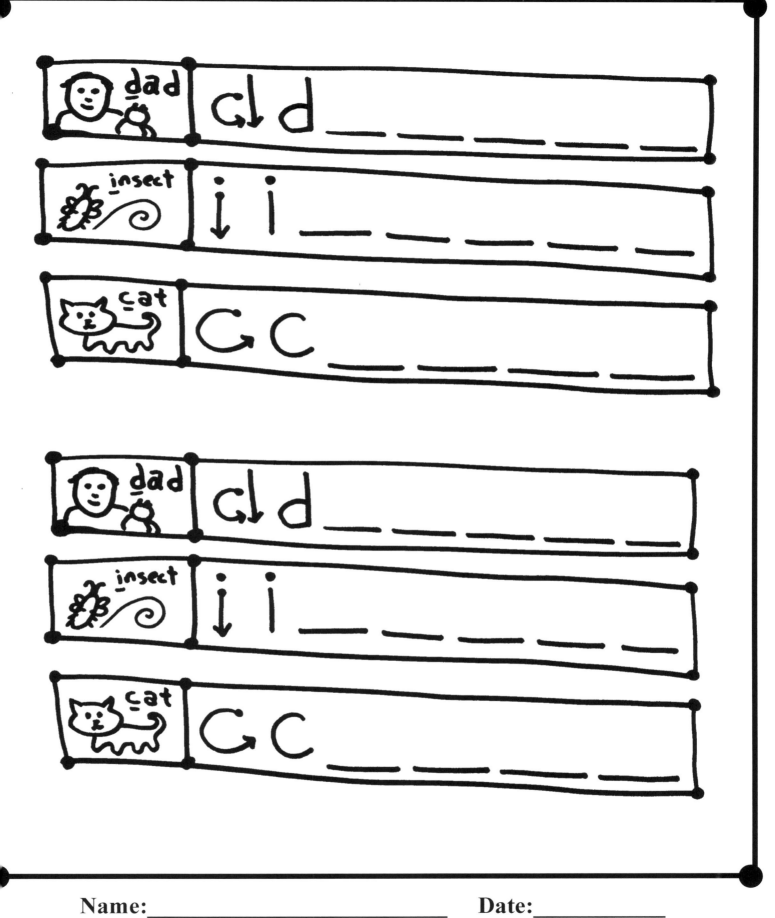

Name: _____ **Date:** _____

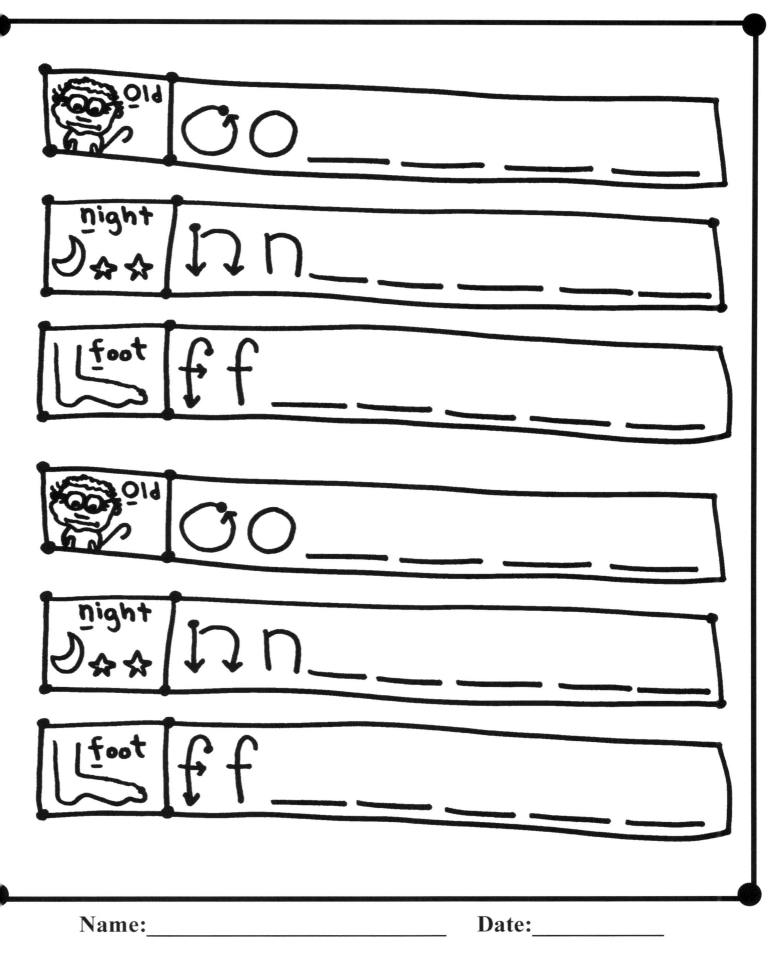

old

night

foot

old

night

foot

Name:_____ **Date:**_____

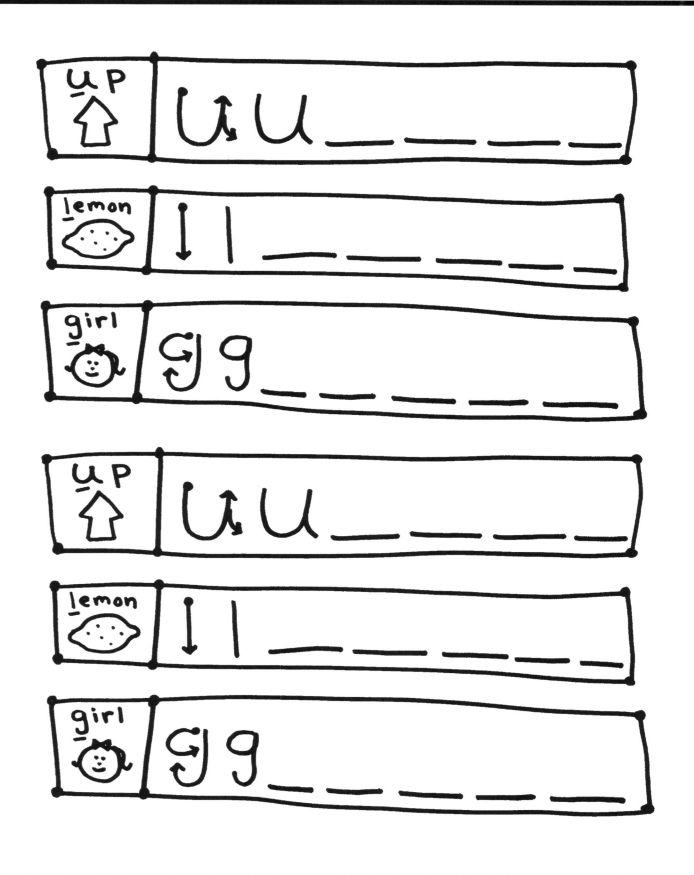

Name:_____ **Date:**_____

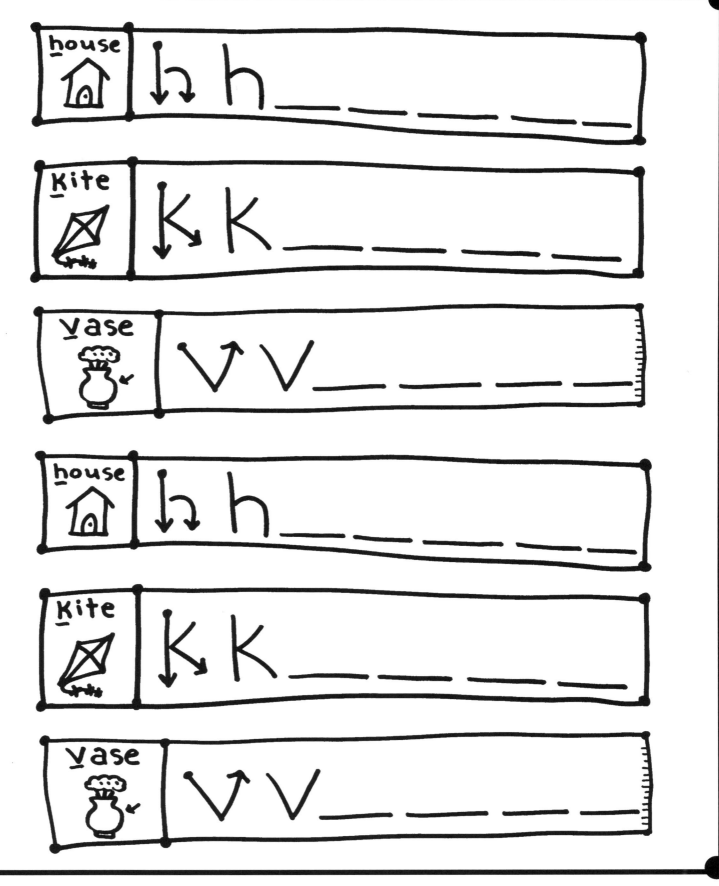

Name:_____   Date:_____

water	W w _ _ _ _
thin	t h t h _ _ _ _
shirt	S h s h _ _ _ _
water	W w _ _ _
thin	t h t h _ _ _ _
shirt	S h s h _ _ _ _

Name:_____ **Date:**_____

Pig

P P _____

church

Ch ch _____

baby

b b _____

Pig

P P _____

church

Ch ch _____

baby

b b _____

Name:_____ Date:_____

Name:_____ **Date:**_____

white

Wh wh _ _ _ _

box

X X _ _ _ _

Zebra

Z z _ _ _ _

queen

Qu qu _ _ _ _

Name:_____   Date:_____

Name:_____   **Date:**_____

Letter Challenge

Certificate of Completion

_____

Name & Age

_____

Date of Completion

The Thinking
TREE

_____

Dyslexia Games ~ Series 3

_____

Teacher

DyslexiaGames.com

Letter Challenge

Art Games, Puzzles & Patterns

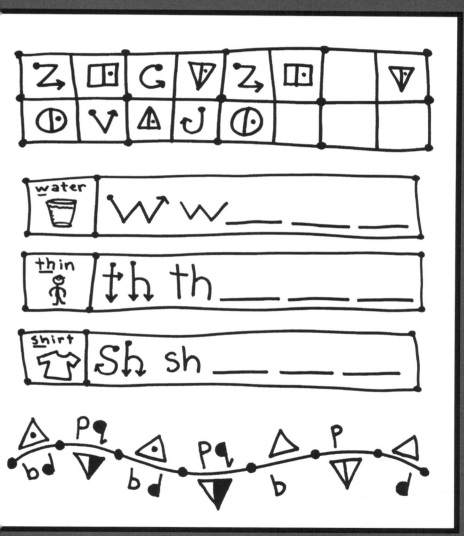

Made in the USA
Columbia, SC
13 December 2024

48022892R00039